CW00727469

The Night-time Adventure Notebook

The Night-time Adventure Notebook

 National Trust

Written by Hannah Jones McVey and Nicole Daw

First published in the United Kingdom in 2015 by
National Trust Books
1 Gower Street, London WC1E 6HD

An imprint of Pavilion Books Group Ltd

The National Trust is a registered charity, no. 205846

Designed for the National Trust by 18 feet and rising. Based on original concept and content by Behaviour Change with design work by N. Duncan Mills.

Photographs: ©National Trust Images/Jonathan Plant 74 (bottom), 82; ©National Trust Images/Steve Sayers 84; ©Alamy/Frankie Angel 51 (top); ©Alamy/Roger Bamber 94; ©Alamy/Dave Bevan 75 (top), 81; ©Alamy/Natasha Bidgood 5; ©Alamy/Cephas Picture Library 38 (top); ©Alamy/Scott Cook Photo Llc 85; ©Alamy/Mikael Damkier 78; ©Alamy/DonSmith 8 (top); ©Alamy/Redmond Durrell 74 (top); ©Alamy/Emilio Ereza 96; ©Alamy/FLPA 77; ©Alamy/David Forster 13 (right); ©Alamy/Tim Gainey 74 (top), 79; ©Alamy/Christin Gasner 7 (right), 62 (middle); ©Alamy/Craig Holmes Premium 2 (middle); ©Alamy/Horizons WWP 11 (top); ©Alamy/Toby Houlton 9 (left); ©Alamy/Chris Howes/Wild Places 74 (bottom); ©Alamy/imageBROKER 6 (top), 14 (middle), 76; ©Alamy/Steve Platzer 12 (middle); ©Alamy/Manor Photography 26 (middle); ©Alamy/OJO Images Ltd 80; ©Alamy/David Robinson, 51 (top); ©Alamy/SDM IMAGES 6 (bottom).

Illustrations by Richard Horne, elhorno.co.uk

ISBN: 978-1-909881-48-8
A CIP catalogue record for this book is available from the British Library.

Reproduction by Mission Productions, Hong Kong
Printed and bound by 1010 Printing International Ltd, China

This book can be ordered direct from the publisher at the website pavilionbooks.com, or try your local bookshop. Also available at National Trust shops and nationaltrustbooks.co.uk

CONTENTS

Introduction 8
Being a night-time commando 10

MAKE

1. Make glow-in-the-dark sugar
2. Cook campfire popcorn
3. Keep a moon chart
4. Have a bonfire
5. Set up a moth trap
6. Hollow out a Punkie Night lantern
7. Create a feast for a hedgehog
8. Make a firelighter
9. Build a woodland lantern
10. Light up a tree

SEE

11. Tell the time using the moon
12. Keep an eye on fungi
13. Go on a bat walk
14. Go on an owl prowl
15. Take a torch to your local pond
16. Stake out a badger sett
17. Find the man in the moon
18. Light up a snow lantern
19. Become a moon gazer
20. Wish on a star

TRY

21. Search for glow worms
22. Go night orienteering
23. Get up for sunrise
24. Sleep under the stars
25. Search for eyes in the dark
26. Enjoy the dawn chorus
27. Have a night from the past
28. Be a night-time scavenger
29. Go wassailing
30. Become a night rider

PLAY

31. Play tapping sticks
32. Become a firefly
33. Play on a moonlit beach
34. Follow a cat
35. Shadow dance in the streetlight
36. Tell stories by firelight
37. Leave a will-o'-the-wisp trail
38. Create a new constellation
39. Make a scary forest
40. Make shadow puppets

EXPERIMENT

41. Keep warm with spiced hot apple juice
42. Have a picnic in the dark
43. Learn Morse code
44. Test your night vision
45. Howl at the full moon
46. Create an ice sculpture
47. Record the sunset
48. Draw a sensory map
49. Plant a night garden
50. Discover a natural night-time wonder

10 best things to do 74

The best things to do throughout the year 86

Introduction

Welcome back to the great outdoors. This time there's an extra challenge – the dark! Put your coat on, grab a torch and get ready for the strange and exciting night-time world. Whether you're at the park, in the woods or in your garden, we have loads of fun things to do after the sun goes down. You'll find strange experiments, crazy games, great things to make and amazing animals to watch. Attract moths, make glow-in-the-dark sugar, spot a shooting star, go night orienteering, cook campfire popcorn, plant a night garden and much more!

We've put together a list of the 50 greatest night-time challenges for you to complete before you're 11¾, and we're making it easy to do them somewhere near you with a little helping hand from the National Trust. In this book, tick them off as you go, write down your notes and stick souvenirs in to remind you of your adventures.

The only question is, can you complete all 50?

Being a night-time commando

The best thing about night-time adventures is that the shadows, sounds and creatures can make you feel like you're on a different planet.

Real success in a new world comes from understanding the things that live there.

Because it's harder to see at night, animals that come out then often have a strong sense of smell. So save your bath until after you have been out on a night-time safari. The animals will smell your bubblebath a mile off!

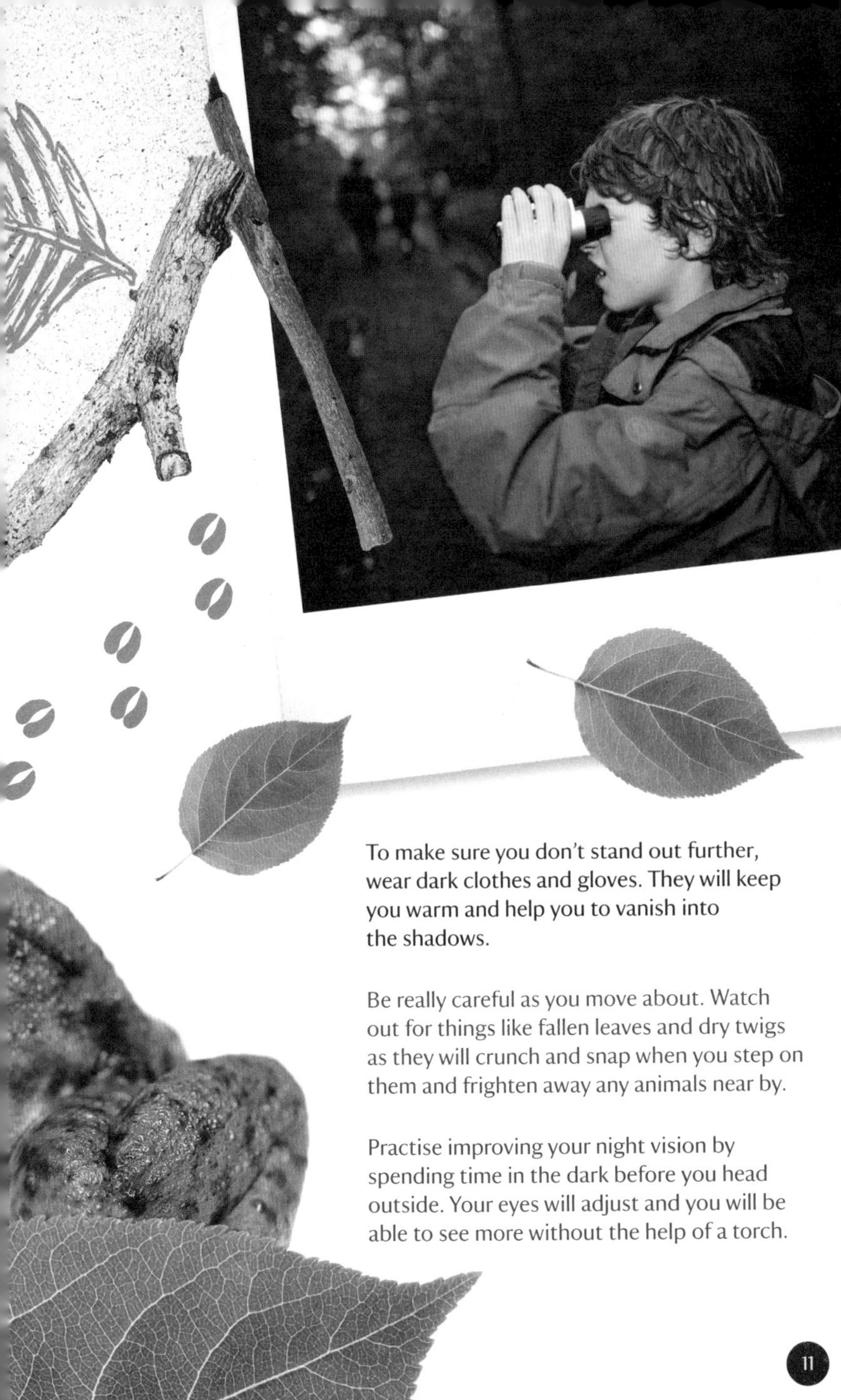

To make sure you don't stand out further, wear dark clothes and gloves. They will keep you warm and help you to vanish into the shadows.

Be really careful as you move about. Watch out for things like fallen leaves and dry twigs as they will crunch and snap when you step on them and frighten away any animals near by.

Practise improving your night vision by spending time in the dark before you head outside. Your eyes will adjust and you will be able to see more without the help of a torch.

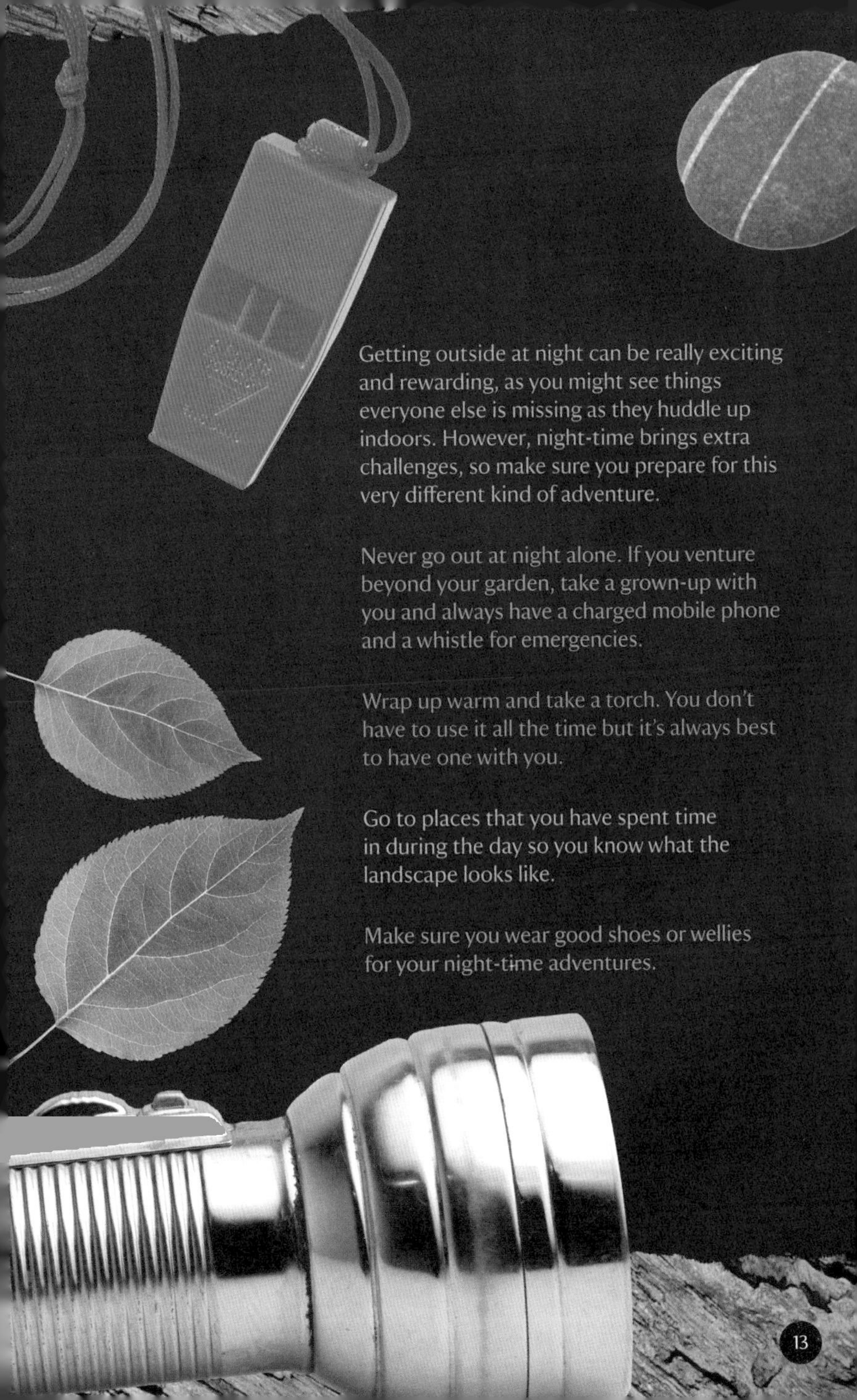

Getting outside at night can be really exciting and rewarding, as you might see things everyone else is missing as they huddle up indoors. However, night-time brings extra challenges, so make sure you prepare for this very different kind of adventure.

Never go out at night alone. If you venture beyond your garden, take a grown-up with you and always have a charged mobile phone and a whistle for emergencies.

Wrap up warm and take a torch. You don't have to use it all the time but it's always best to have one with you.

Go to places that you have spent time in during the day so you know what the landscape looks like.

Make sure you wear good shoes or wellies for your night-time adventures.

MAKE

1. Make glow-in-the-dark sugar ☐
2. Cook campfire popcorn ☐
3. Keep a moon chart ☐
4. Have a bonfire ☐
5. Set up a moth trap ☐
6. Hollow out a Punkie Night lantern ☐
7. Create a feast for a hedgehog ☐
8. Make a firelighter ☐
9. Build a woodland lantern ☐
10. Light up a tree ☐

1

Make glow-in-the-dark sugar

Discover triboluminescence

What you need:

- Sugar cubes
- A flat surface
- A flat-bottomed glass (an empty jam jar will do)

Find a really dark place and have a go at crushing sugar cubes under a flat-bottomed glass. You should see flashes of blue light as the sugar crumbles. Triboluminescence means 'rubbing light' and happens when certain materials are rubbed or ripped.

Top tip!

Your eyes need to adjust to the light to see these flashes at their best, so make sure it is very dark and that you have sat there for a while.

Find a crayon, oil pastel or scrap from a magazine that matches the colour of the flash and scribble or stick it here:

Date completed: Day ________ Month ______________ Year ___________

2 Cook campfire popcorn

Enjoy this amazing campfire snack

What you need:

- Popping corn
- Good-quality tin foil
- Cooking oil
- A campfire (see page 19)
- A long cooking fork
- A grown-up to help you
- Flavourings

Put 4 teaspoons of uncooked popping corn and 2 teaspoons of oil in the middle of a square piece of foil. Scrunch the foil into a parcel, making sure you leave a big space for the popcorn to explode into. Poke the cooking fork prongs into the top of the foil pack and ask an adult to lift it gently onto hot coals or embers. When they hear the first pop they should lift the package above the heat and shake gently until the popping stops. Place it on a heatproof surface and wait for the foil to cool before unwrapping and eating.

Top tip!

You can add flavouring to your popcorn after it has popped to make it even more delicious. Get creative: butter, cocoa, salt, garlic, herbs ... it may not work but it's fun to experiment!

What were your favourite flavourings?

Date completed: Day ________ Month ______________ Year ___________

3

Keep a moon chart

What shape will the moon be tonight?

What you need:

- Black paper
- Chalk

We see different parts of the moon as it moves round the earth. Mark each day of the month out on a black piece of paper, leaving room for your moon drawing next to each day. Every night use your chalk to draw the shape of the moon and watch it slowly change shape.

Top tip!

Doing this in the winter will mean you see the moon earlier in the evening.

What is your favourite shaped moon? Draw it here

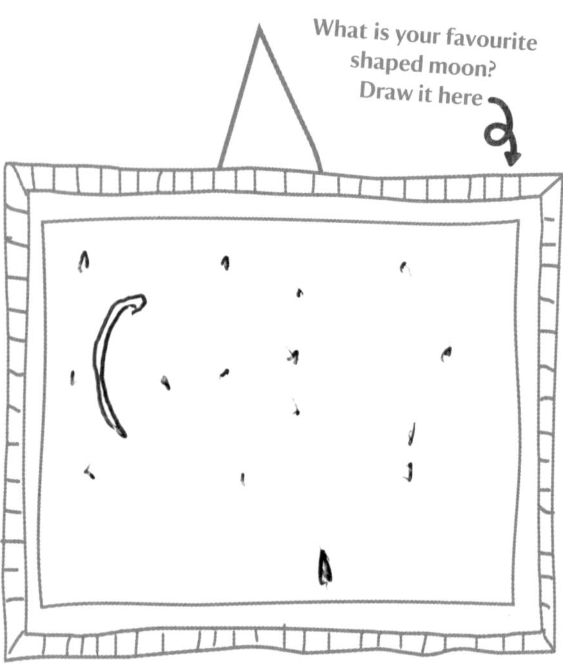

Date completed: Day ________ Month ________________ Year ____________

4

Have a bonfire

No cold night is complete without a bonfire

What you need:

- A safe space
- Things to burn (dry wood, kindling and small sticks)
- A grown-up to help you and some friends
- A bucket of sand or water

Top tip!

Make the fire as close to when you plan to light it as possible so that there is no time for small creatures like hedgehogs to move in.

Find a site away from buildings, trees and plants. Dig a pit about 5cm deep and a half a metre wider than you want your fire to be. Put bricks or heavy logs all around the edges. Build up tinder (twigs, bark, grass, dried leaves) in a tepee shape in the middle of the pit, leaving a small gap on one side so that a natural firelighter (see page 23) can be placed in the centre. Add some small twigs (kindling), leaving a gap in the same place. Lay four layers of medium-sized sticks on top and large logs around the base. Ask a grown-up to light the firelighter and push it into the gap to the centre of the bonfire with a stick. When you're finished put the fire out completely with water or sand and pile dirt on top afterwards.

Try toasting marshmallows with sticks over the fire. Who ate the most?

Date completed: Day ________ Month ________________ Year ____________

Set up a moth trap

Discover the incredible moths that only come out at night

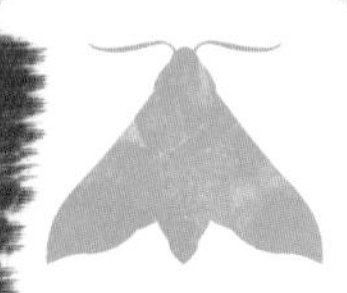

What you need:

- A white sheet
- A good torch
- String or rope

Most moths fly at night and they are attracted to light. You can make your own trap by hanging a white sheet in your garden, park or local wild space and shining a bright torch onto it. The longer you leave the light the more moths will come.

Top tip!

To look closely at a moth, put it into a clear plastic or glass container and avoid touching the wings. Put it back near to where you found it so it can find its way home.

How many moths did you see?

Date completed: Day ________ Month ______________ Year ___________

6

Hollow out a Punkie Night lantern

Have a go at making this traditional turnip light

What you need:

- A turnip
- A metal spoon
- A tea light

Punkie Night is an old Somerset tradition that is celebrated on the last Thursday of October. Hollow out a turnip using your spoon until only a thin layer is left. Put your tea light through the hole in the top and the light will glow eerily through the skin of the turnip.

Try using other vegetables as lanterns, such as peppers and potatoes. Record your successes ... and failures here:

Top tip!

Turnips are really hard so you may find it easier to ask a grown-up to help you hollow it out using a power drill.

Did you know?

Lanterns were also made using mangelwurzels, a root vegetable usually grown for cow food.

Date completed: Day ________ Month ________________ Year ____________

7

Create a feast for a hedgehog

Make a mouthwatering feast for the hedgehogs in your garden

What you need:

- Shallow bowls
- Tinned dog or cat food (not fish-based)
- Chopped boiled eggs
- Water

Hedgehogs mainly eat bugs like earwigs and beetles. To tempt them into your garden, fill shallow bowls with dog or cat food or chopped boiled eggs. Never feed hedgehogs milk as it will upset their stomachs. Put the bowls in a quiet part of the garden and watch from the window to see if visitors arrive.

Top tip!

Don't leave the food there permanently as it may attract other creatures that you don't want to have in your garden.

Write out your menu for a hedgehog below:

MENU

starter fruit and veg ~~carrot and cucumbe~~

main course

pudding muffin

Date completed: Day ________ Month ________________ Year ____________

8 Make a firelighter

An easy way to get your bonfire off to a roaring start

What you need:

- A pine cone
- Some string
- A couple of old candles
- A saucepan
- Water
- An empty golden syrup tin or similar
- A baking tray
- An oven
- A baking sheet

Top tip!

Coat the baking sheet with glitter and roll the pine cone around to give your firelighter an extra shine.

Dry your pine cone for two hours in an oven on a low temperature. Place the tin in a saucepan full of hot water. Put the candles in the tin until they melt, then move the pan to a heatproof surface. Tie a length of string to the top of the cone then dip it into the wax so that the cone and 2cm of string are covered. Put it onto a baking sheet to dry and cool, then cut the string where the wax ends. When you are ready to light your bonfire, light the string and put the pine cone in the fire.

Date completed: Day ________ Month ________________ Year ____________

9 Make a woodland lantern

Light up the darkness with these beautiful lanterns

What you need:

- Eight 1cm thick, straight sticks
- String or masking tape
- Pale-coloured tissue paper
- PVA glue mixed with a little water
- Paint brush and pot
- A pair of scissors
- Dry woodland treasures eg leaves, flowers and feathers
- A tea light candle
- An adult to help you

Follow the diagram to make the frame of the lantern. Use string or tape to attach the sticks. Cut two triangles of tissue paper for each side of the lantern (3cm bigger all round). Cover each piece of tissue paper with glue. Sandwich a couple of woodland treasures in the middle of the pieces. Paint more glue on your sticks and attach the triangles, curling the extra tissue paper round the sticks. Let the tissue paper dry then place a tea light on a fireproof flat surface and ask a grown-up to light it for you. Place your lantern over the top and see your creation come to life.

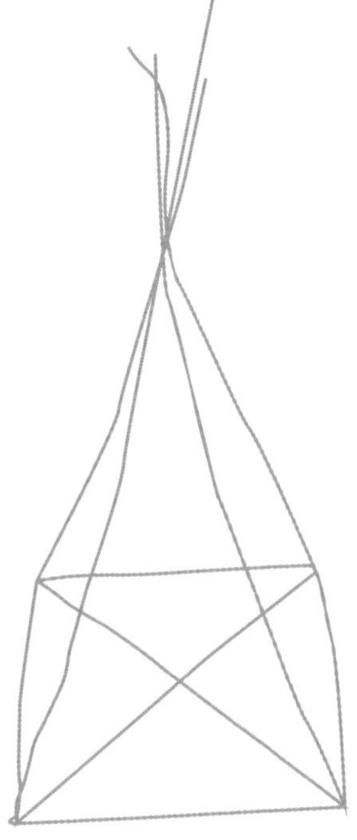

What woodland treasures did you add?

Date completed: Day ________ Month ________________ Year ____________

10

Light up a tree

Show off your favourite tree

What you need:

- A tree
- Torches
- A bucket of sand

Top tip!

Put different-coloured tissue paper over the torch light for a more magical display.

Choose your favourite tree in your garden, local park or wood. By pointing torches upwards at the tree you can show off the shapes of its branches. Putting the torches in a bucket of sand will make this easier.

Which tree did you choose to light up and why?

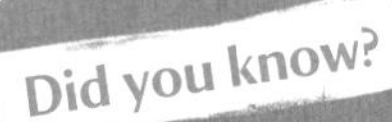

Did you know?

If the tree is Christmas tree-shaped, putting the torch further away from the trunk will light up more of the branches.

Date completed: Day ________ Month ________________ Year ____________

SEE

11. Tell the time using the moon ☐
12. Keep an eye on fungi ☐
13. Go on a bat walk ☐
14. Go on an owl prowl ☐
15. Take a torch to your local pond ☐
16. Stake out a badger sett ☐
17. Find the man in the moon ☐
18. Light up a snow lantern ☐
19. Become a moon gazer ☐
20. Wish on a star ☐

11

Tell the time using the moon

Some tips for telling the time when the moon is out

What you need:

- A good view of a full moon
- A compass

The moon rises in the east and sets in the west. At full moon you can guess the time by looking to see how high it is in the sky. The highest point will be around midnight. Halfway between this point and the horizon in the east it will be 9pm, and half way between its highest point and the horizon in the west it will be 3am.

Use this diagram to help you. Hold it up to the night sky and mark the position of the moon:

Top tip!

If you are by the sea you can watch the tides being controlled by the position of the moon. High tide is six hours after low tide, so if you know what time the sea was at its lowest and how far the water comes up the beach at high tide you can make a good guess at the time.

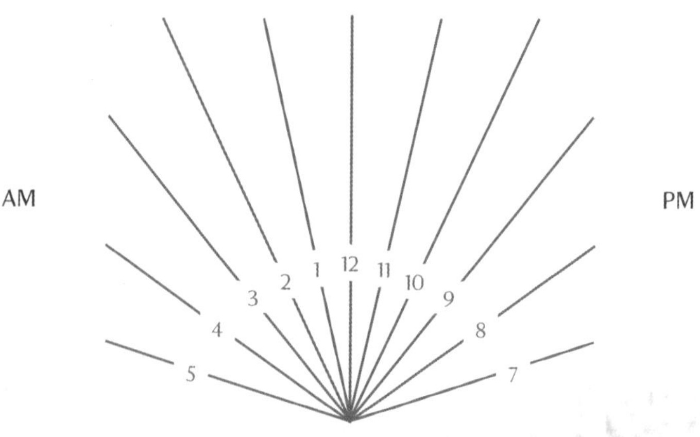

Date completed: Day ________ Month ________________ Year ____________

Keep an eye on fungi

Watch carefully or they will disappear!

What you need:

- A notebook
- Somewhere that fungi love – a damp log or woodland undergrowth are good places to look

Fungi often pop up overnight and can disappear quickly too. Go for a walk – autumn is best – just before dark and note down all the fungi you see. Do the same each night for a week and see how quickly they pop up and how they change each day.

Top tip!

In the summer a shaggy inkcap is a great one to spot. They have a long white shaggy head and are often seen in grassy areas. They will often appear after a soggy night and will slowly shrivel up into a black inky pulp over the next few days.

Stick pictures of some of the fungi you see here:

Did you know?

Some fungi are very poisonous, so unless you are with an expert who can tell what each fungi is it is best not to touch them.

Date completed: Day ________ Month ______________ Year ____________

13 Go on a bat walk

Find a local group and discover bats close to your home

What you need:

- Warm clothes
- A torch, ideally with a red light (a red sweet wrapper tied over with an elastic band would do)
- A bat detector (not essential)

Bats spend most of the winter hibernating, so April to September will be the best time for your bat walk. Local experts regularly run events and will have special equipment to help you hear their ultra high-pitched calls.

Top tip!

International Bat Night is on the last weekend in August. This is a great time to find a local event and a good excuse to stay up late!

Use this space to draw a picture of the bats you saw or heard on your bat walk

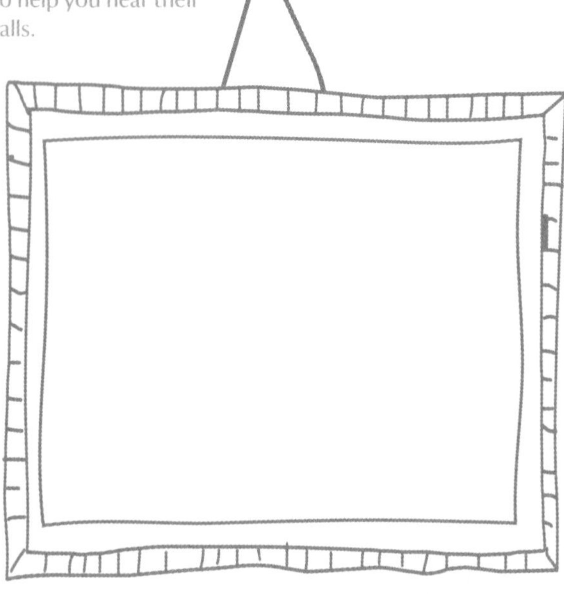

Date completed: Day ________ Month ______________ Year ___________

14 Go on an owl prowl

Keep your ears and eyes peeled for these amazing night-time birds

What you need:

- Warm clothes
- A torch, ideally with a red light (a red sweet wrapper tied over with an elastic band would do)
- Your best owl call

Most owls are nocturnal animals, coming out at night to hunt and socialise. Seeing owls is tricky, but you can often hear tawny owls twit-twooing at night in woodlands and parks. If you can copy the call, you might get an owl calling in response.

Take a photo of you and your friends on your owl prowl and stick it here:

Top tip!

Red torch beams and lights are thought to be almost invisible to night-time creatures, so they don't scare them away.

Date completed: Day ________ Month ______________ Year ___________

15

Take a torch to your local pond

What's going on underwater in the dark?

What you need:

- Warm clothes
- A torch with a strong beam
- An identification book/chart (optional)
- A wildlife pond

Newts, frogs and toads are nocturnal animals and can be found in ponds in the spring. Stand near a pond, keeping clear of the edge, and move your torch beam slowly over the surface of the water. As your eyes adapt, you will see creatures swimming or motionless in the water.

As well as newts and frogs, there may be insects such as water boatmen, pond skaters and dragonfly nymphs.

Top tip!

The best time to look for newts, frogs and toads is between March and May on a warm, still evening.

Write a list of what you saw here:

Date completed: Day ________ Month ______________ Year __________

16

Stake out a badger sett

You'll have to be quiet to spot these secretive animals

What you need:

- Dark warm clothes that don't rustle
- Good listening skills
- Patience
- Something comfy to sit on
- A torch, ideally with a red light (a red sweet wrapper tied over with an elastic band would do)

Top tip!

Badgers have an excellent sense of smell. Make sure you wait downwind of the sett and don't use any strong-smelling soap or toiletries before going out.

During the day, badgers stay in their underground homes, called setts. Once you know where a sett is you have a good chance of seeing badgers there at night. Find a comfy spot to sit at least an hour before dark. It is best to rest against a tree or other natural feature and stay very still so you don't stick out.

How many badgers did you see?

Did you know?

In the summer badgers often come out before it is dark. So make sure you approach the sett very quietly.

Date completed: Day ________ Month ______________ Year ____________

Find the man in the moon

Can you see his face?

What you need:

- A clear night with a full moon

Look at the top right of a full moon to see the right eye and then find the left eye in the dark patch to the left. The moon has a surprised expression, so look for an 'O'- shaped mouth, a little curved nose and raised eyebrows. Can you see other faces hidden in the light and dark parts of the moon's surface?

Top tip!

The moon's face is easiest to see at twilight when it glows less.

Draw a picture of the face you saw in the moon here:

Date completed: Day ________ Month ________________ Year ____________

Light up a snow lantern

These traditional Swedish lanterns look wonderful in the garden on a cold snowy night

What you need:

- Snow
- A candle (a candle holder is handy)
- Matches
- Gloves
- A grown-up to help you

Take a candle and place it on a flat patch of snow. Use a candle holder or pack some snow around the candle to make sure it stands up straight. Make ten large snowballs (about the size of a grown-up's fist) and place them in a circle around the candle with their sides touching. Make ten more and place each of those on a new layer above the first ring, each one bridging the gaps across the layer below.

Use black paper and chalk to draw a picture of your lanterns and stick it here:

Top tip!

Tap each snowball very gently on the top to help it stay in place.

Date completed: Day ________ Month ______________ Year ____________

Become a moon gazer

Try out this ancient way of meditating

What you need:

- Warm clothes
- A quiet place

Stare at the moon until you need to close your eyes. When you close them you will see the white circle of the moon on the inside of your eyelids. Concentrate on that until it disappears. If you practise, the image will stay for longer each time.

Top tip!

Make yourself really comfortable when you try out this exercise. The more relaxed you are, the easier it will be.

How many seconds could you hold the shape of the moon on your eyelids after closing your eyes?

Did you know?

This is an ancient yoga technique called Tratka. It is believed that it will increase the power of your brain!

Date completed: Day ________ Month ______________ Year ___________

Wish on a star

What will you wish for?

What you need:

- A clear night sky
- A wish

People disagree which is the best star to make a wish on. Some believe it must be a shooting star, some the brightest star, and others think it's the first one to appear in the night sky. It's probably best to try all of them just in case.

Top tip!

There are over 100 dark sky discovery locations in the UK. These are fantastic places to see stars, so look up your local one at darkskydiscovery.org.uk.

What stars did you wish on?

Date completed: Day __________ Month __________________ Year ______________

TRY

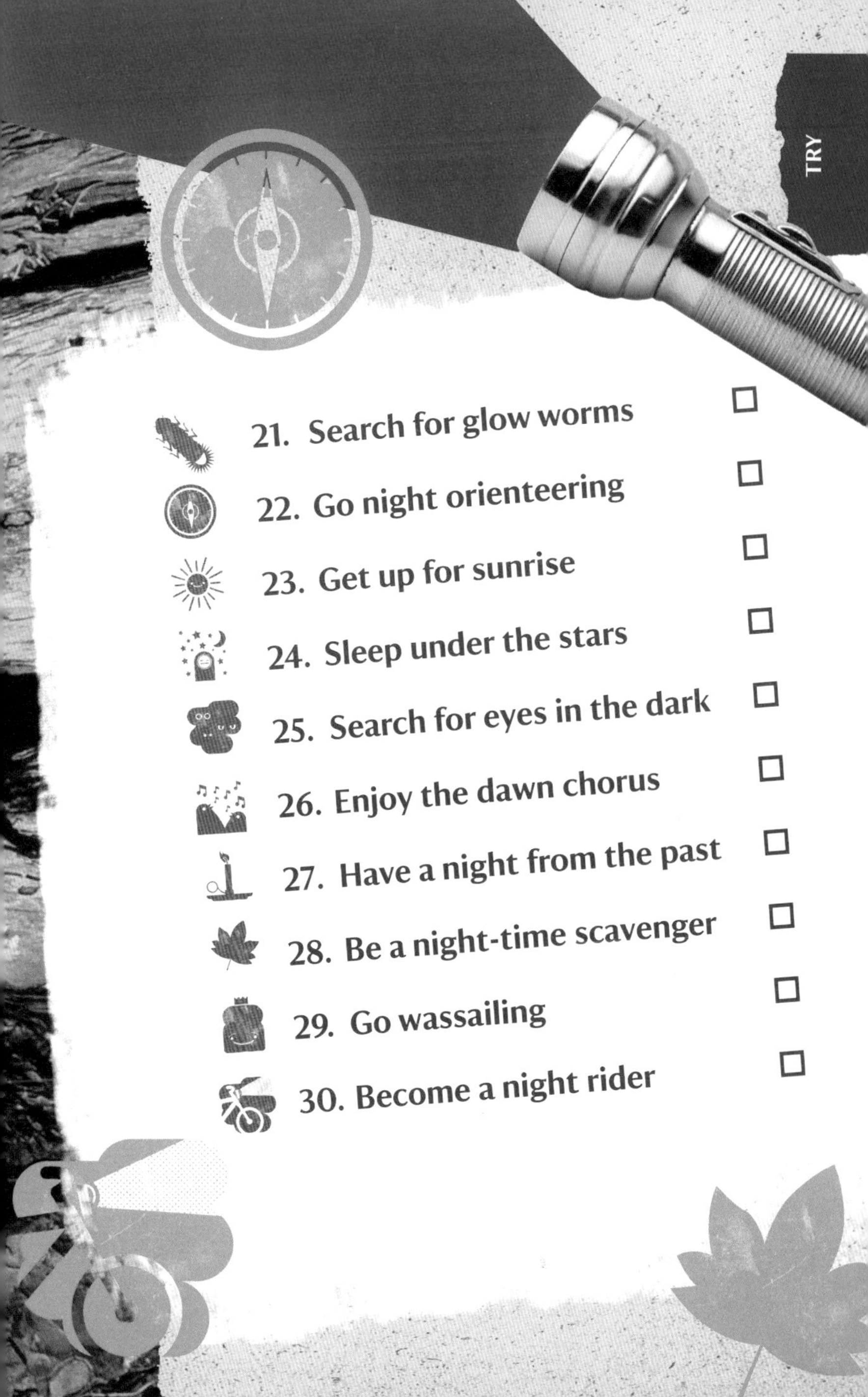

21. Search for glow worms ☐
22. Go night orienteering ☐
23. Get up for sunrise ☐
24. Sleep under the stars ☐
25. Search for eyes in the dark ☐
26. Enjoy the dawn chorus ☐
27. Have a night from the past ☐
28. Be a night-time scavenger ☐
29. Go wassailing ☐
30. Become a night rider ☐

21

Search for glow worms

Find these natural fairy lights

What you need:

- A torch

Glow worms in the UK are actually small beetles. The females glow to attract a mate. Glow worms can be found in all kinds of open places, including gardens, woodland and disused railway lines, especially in Wiltshire, Dorset and the South Downs.

Top tip!

The glowing season runs from May to September and is at its peak in June and July. The National Trust runs glow worm walks occasionally. Search nationaltrust.org.uk for details.

Where did you see the most glow worms?

Date completed: Day ________ Month ________________ Year ____________

Go night orienteering

Rely on your compass to get you through the darkness

What you need:

- Map
- Compass
- A good torch
- A team of family or friends

Orienteering at night is a really adventurous challenge. For your first time choose a short route you know well and make sure you know how to use your map and compass. Be sure to stick with your group.

Top tip!

Head torches are really useful for night orienteering. With your torch on your head, everywhere you look is lit and you have your hands free for using your map and compass.

Draw the route you completed here. Be sure to add any interesting features you saw along the way:

Date completed: Day ________ Month ________________ Year ______________

23 Get up for sunrise

Watch the world waking up

What you need:

- Warm clothes
- An alarm clock

Sunrise is a very special time of the day, but not one that many people see. In the summer sunrise is much earlier – sometimes as early as three in the morning! In the winter it can be as late as eight. Dress up warm and enjoy the world getting ready for a new day.

Top tip!

Check the internet or a newspaper to find out exactly what time sunrise is each day. Make sure you are up a little earlier so you can enjoy the whole spectacle.

Show on this clock what time sunrise was the day you watched.

Date completed: Day ________ Month ________________ Year ____________

24

Sleep under the stars

A really special experience

What you need:

- Warm clothes
- A good sleeping bag
- A place to sleep (only do this activity in your garden with a grown-up or with a trained grown-up in a safe place)
- A plastic sheet (optional)

Sleeping under the stars is the perfect way to experience the night sky. Wrap up warm and snuggle in. String a plastic sheet up if you are worried about rain, but it is best to head out on a warm summer's night when you can enjoy the stars until the moment you close your eyes.

Top tip!

You might want to make a bonfire in the evening to keep warm. Make sure you do not sleep too close to the fire and that it is under control before anyone goes to sleep.

Where did you sleep out? Write about your experiences here:

Date completed: Day ________ Month ________________ Year ____________

25

Search for eyes in the dark

What is staring back at you?

What you need:

- A torch, ideally with a red light (a red sweet wrapper tied over with an elastic band would do)

Many animals have something called a *tapedum lucidum* in their eye that helps them to see better in the dark. Different animals' eyes glow different colours. Foxes' eyes glow red, spiders' eyes glow blue and green and some dogs' eyes glow a turquoise colour.

Draw the eyes that you saw. What colours were they?

Top tip!

Dogs, cats, sheep, cows and pigs – one of these animals doesn't have glowing eyes. Have a game to see if you can find out which one by carefully shining your torch from a distance.

Date completed: Day ________ Month ________________ Year ____________

26

Enjoy the dawn chorus

Get up early to hear bird song at its best

What you need:

- Warm clothes
- Good listening skills
- Binoculars (optional)

Go out just before sunrise, or perhaps camp overnight. Different kinds of birds will start singing at different times. The first to start singing are blackbirds, robins and wrens. Once you can hear birds singing you can use your binoculars to try to spot them.

How many different bird calls did you hear?

Top tip!

The dawn chorus is at its best in spring when birds sing to attract a mate or to protect their territory.

Date completed: Day ________ Month ______________ Year ___________

27 Have a night from the past

What will you do with no electricity?

What you need:

- A good imagination
- Some candles and matches

The lightbulb was invented in Victorian times. Before then homes were lit with candles or oil lamps and there were no TVs, computers or tablets to entertain people in the evenings. Challenge your family to a night from the past by turning off electrical lights and gadgets and entertaining yourselves by candlelight.

Top tip!

Try playing board games or reading a book out loud.

Write a diary of the night you turned off the power here:

Date completed: Day ________ Month ________________ Year ____________

28 Be a night-time scavenger

Scavenger hunts are much harder at night than in daylight

What you need:

- Warm clothes
- A torch
- A list of things to hunt for
- A bag to collect them in

Top tip!

Remember not to pick wild flowers or berries unless you are sure what they are.

Hunting for a list of items is good fun during the day, but night-time brings an extra challenge.

Can you find?

- A leaf that makes a good shadow
- A wand-shaped stick
- Something white (white things are easier to see in the dark)
- A fairy's bed

Draw the leaf that makes the best shadow here:

Date completed: Day ________ Month ________________ Year ____________

29

Go wassailing

Feeding toast to a tree?! Enjoy this West Country tradition

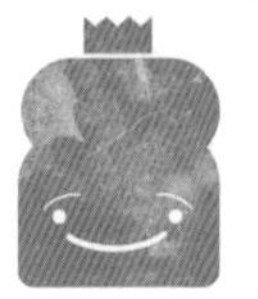

What you need:

- An orchard or fruit tree
- Some toast
- String
- Pots, pans and spoons
- Some fun songs that everyone knows
- A group of friends or family

Wassailing is an ancient winter tradition in places where people grow apples for cider. To scare off bad spirits and ensure a good harvest they sing, bang pots and pans and hang toast from the branches of the apple trees to feed them! Pick a Wassail King and Queen to lead you.

Make up your own song (called a wassail) to encourage the tree to have a good year and write it here so you can teach it to your friends:

Top tip!

You can finish your wassail with a bonfire (see page 19) and storytelling (see page 57) for a really magical night.

Date completed: Day ________ Month ________________ Year ____________

30 Become a night rider

Find somewhere to ride your bike at night

What you need:

- A bike
- Bike lights at the front and back
- Reflective clothing
- A helmet
- A grown-up

Riding at night means you have to be even more alert. Imagine you are an urban fox navigating the streets in the dark. At first, cycle a traffic-free route that you know well. See how different it feels when you can only see what is lit up by your bike light.

What did you see on your ride that you hadn't noticed during the day? Write or draw it here:

Top tip!

Start your ride at dusk, just before night starts to fall. Cycle to somewhere you know well and then retrace your route in the dark. That way you will know what to expect.

Date completed: Day ________ Month ________________ Year ____________

PLAY

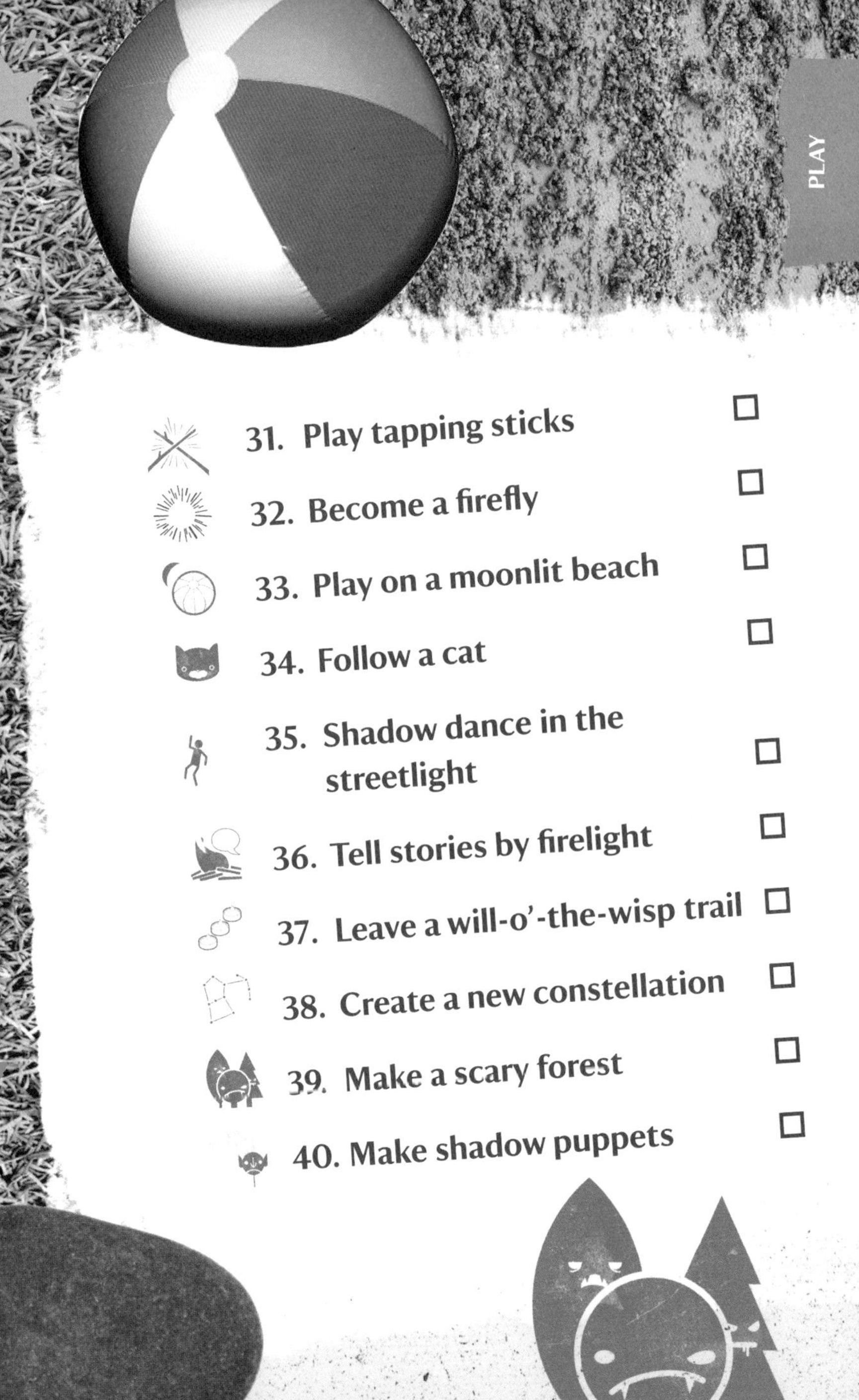

31. Play tapping sticks ☐
32. Become a firefly ☐
33. Play on a moonlit beach ☐
34. Follow a cat ☐
35. Shadow dance in the streetlight ☐
36. Tell stories by firelight ☐
37. Leave a will-o'-the-wisp trail ☐
38. Create a new constellation ☐
39. Make a scary forest ☐
40. Make shadow puppets ☐

31 Play tapping sticks

Hide and seek with a night-time twist

What you need:

- Warm clothes
- Two sticks
- An outdoor space

Playing hide and seek at night means you cannot rely on your eyes to do the finding. This version is perfect because it uses your ears instead. The hider taps two sticks together every few seconds once they have found their hiding place. The seeker can then use the sound to find them.

How did hiding in the dark make you feel? Write some words or draw a picture here to describe your feelings:

Top tip!

If you play in an area with lots of buildings or in a valley your tapping sticks might echo, which will really confuse the seeker!

Date completed: Day ________ Month ______________ Year ___________

Become a firefly

Watch out for the flickering lights

What you need:

- A torch per person
- A safe place to run around

Give everyone a torch and play a game of firefly tag in the dark. The catcher can shout 'FIREFLY' whenever they want. When they do, everyone with a torch (the fireflies) must flash it on and off once. Using these signals, the catcher has to find and capture a firefly, who then becomes the catcher.

Can you think of a new rule to add to this game? Write it here and have a go with your friends:

Top tip!

Flash your torch above your head or down near the ground in order to confuse the catcher.

Date completed: Day _________ Month _________________ Year ______________

33

Play on a moonlit beach

Enjoy the beach in a new way

What you need:

- A beach
- A good game to play

At full moon the light reflects on the sea, making the beach a surprisingly bright place to be. Head to the beach when the tide is out and enjoy a late-night game of rounders, football or tag.

Top tip!

Get big bottles full of water and attach a head torch to each with the light facing inwards to make glow-in-the-dark goalposts.

Use black paper and chalk to draw a picture of you playing on the beach and stick it here:

Date completed: Day ________ Month ______________ Year __________

Follow a cat

What does your cat get up to at night?

What you need:

- A cat to follow
- A torch
- Sensible shoes and warm clothes

Cats are most active at night. Whilst you are asleep it is likely that your cat is busy hunting, prowling and defending its territory. Follow your cat on its night-time wander and see how far you can get. Don't follow it into people's gardens or anywhere which may be unsafe.

Where did your cat visit? Where was its favourite place?

Top tip!

Use a camera and a torch to create a night-time nature documentary about your cat with you as the presenter.

Date completed: Day ________ Month ________________ Year ____________

Shadow dance in the streetlight

Use these pools of light to create your own shadow dance

What you need:

- A safe pavement with streetlights
- Your dancing shoes

Pools of light created by streetlights on pavements and in parks are the perfect places to show off your shadow and shimmy in the spotlight. Watch your shadow cast different shapes – make yourself tall and thin, spread out like a star and try twirling so fast your shadow becomes a blur.

Draw your shadow dancing in this pool of light:

Top tip!

Try working with friends to make two- or three-person patterns with your bodies or a synchronised dance show.

Date completed: Day ________ Month ________________ Year ____________

Tell stories by firelight

Are you listening carefully? Then I'll begin…

What you need:

- A bonfire (see page 19)
- Friends and families
- A great story to tell

Telling stories around a fire is a wonderful way to spend a dark evening. You can either think up a new story or retell one of your favourites. Remember to use actions and voices to make it more exciting for others. From ghost stories to grand adventure tales, get a story ready in your mind and off you go!

Top tip!

If you feel nervous, just stare into the fire and pretend you are telling it to the flames and that no one else is there.

Who told the best story? Write your favourite bit here:

Date completed: Day ________ Month ________________ Year ____________

37

Leave a will-o'-the-wisp trail

Follow the flickering lights

What you need:

– Tea lights (battery-powered would be best) or torches

In folk tales a will-o'-the-wisp is a ghostly light that leads travellers along a path. Some believe they are dangerous and get people lost, others think they lead to treasure. Place tea lights so that each is just visible from the last and invite your friends to follow your trail.

Is your will-o'-the-wisp a good spirit or a cheeky one who wants to confuse your friends? Draw a picture below of what you think it looks like:

Top tip!

Battery-powered tea lights are safer and won't be blown out by a gust of wind.

Date completed: Day ________ Month ________________ Year ____________

38

Create a new constellation

What's the story behind your stars?

What you need:

- Tea lights
- Matches
- A clear night sky
- A grown-up to help you

Imagine the stars are a dot-to-dot picture. Find a shape – an animal, an object, a face – and use tea lights to mark it out on the ground. Carefully light the tea lights and see your star shape (called a constellation) come to life.

Top tip!

The glow from street lights can make it hard to sees stars in towns and cities. For the best constellation spotting you will need to head out to the countryside far away from lights.

What's the story of your constellation? How did that person, animal or object come to be in the stars?

Date completed: Day ________ Month ______________ Year ___________

39

Make a scary forest

Get ready for a scary night-time walk

What you need:

- Clay
- Things found on the woodland floor such as twigs and leaves
- A torch

Smooth lumps of clay into the bark of trees and attach sticks and funny-shaped leaves to make strange faces with big eyes or long noses. Bring your friends to your scary woods, lighting the way with a torch so that the light eerily reflects the trees as they appear to come alive.

Top tip!

Make spider shapes by tying four sticks together in the centre and hanging it from a tree for an extra scare factor.

Draw the outline of your scariest face here:

Date completed: Day __________ Month ________________ Year ____________

40

Make shadow puppets

Create your own outdoor theatre

Top tip!

Remember that all you will see is the outline, so try and include clear features like a long, crooked nose for a witch.

What you need:

- A torch
- Black card
- Pencil (or chalk may be better for seeing on the black paper)
- Sticks
- A pair of scissors
- Sticky tape
- A clear wall or a big piece of white paper

Draw the outline of a character on a piece of black card. Cut the shape out and attach it to a stick. Hold the puppet by the stick up in front of a wall or big piece of paper. Ask someone to shine a torch at your puppet and a shadow will appear on the wall.

Who were the characters in your play?

Date completed: Day ________ Month ______________ Year ____________

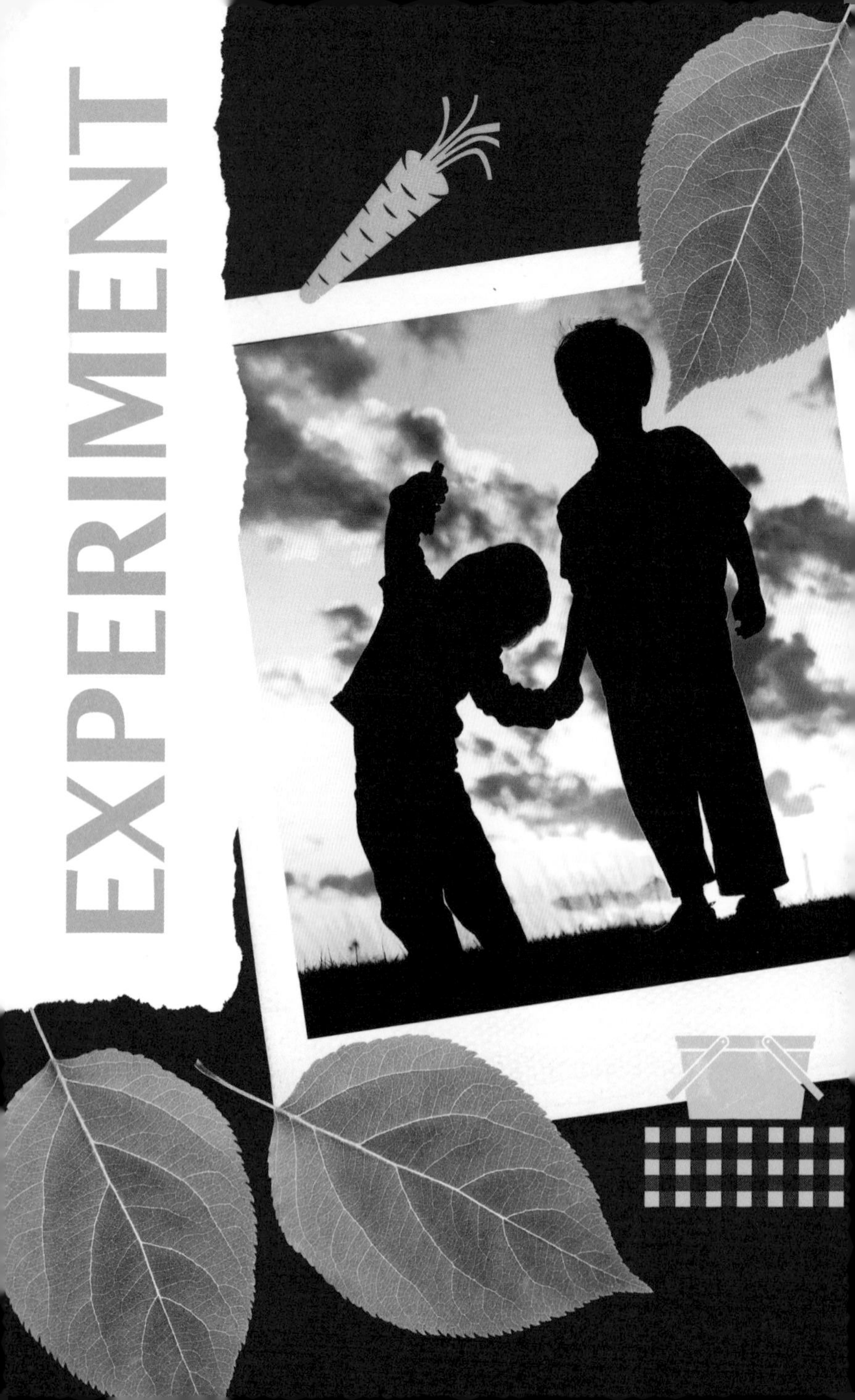
EXPERIMENT

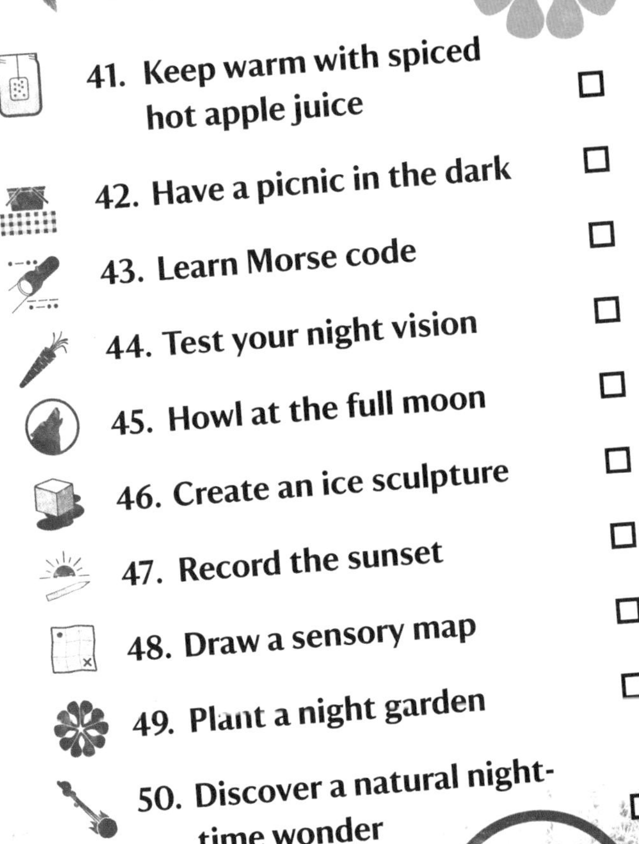

41. Keep warm with spiced hot apple juice ☐
42. Have a picnic in the dark ☐
43. Learn Morse code ☐
44. Test your night vision ☐
45. Howl at the full moon ☐
46. Create an ice sculpture ☐
47. Record the sunset ☐
48. Draw a sensory map ☐
49. Plant a night garden ☐
50. Discover a natural night-time wonder ☐

41

Keep warm with spiced hot apple juice

A perfect fireside drink

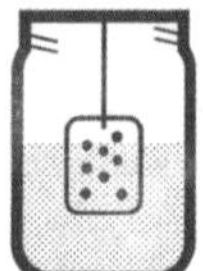

What you need:

- A saucepan
- Apple juice
- A tea bag
- String
- A pair of scissors
- Ground cinnamon, ginger and nutmeg
- A grown-up

Pour your apple juice into a saucepan and put it on a camping stove, hob or the grate across a fire pit. Cut a corner off a tea bag and replace the tea with a pinch of cinnamon, ginger and nutmeg. Tie the corner up with the string. Put the little bag of flavours in the apple juice and wait for it to boil before carefully serving it up.

Top tip!

Orange slices and cloves would make great additions to your apple juice too.

What was the best recipe that you found?

Date completed: Day ________ Month ______________ Year ___________

42

Have a picnic in the dark

A midnight feast with a difference

What you need:

- Warm clothes
- A torch with a strong beam
- Food

Eating in the dark is very strange ... If you can't see, you use your other senses more. You notice the sound your food makes, for example, and it might even taste different! Gather together provisions for your special picnic and head out at night to put this to the test.

Top tip!

Tests have shown that people can enjoy foods they don't usually like when they eat them in the dark. Dare your friends to try sprouts, marmite and pickle to see if they taste different during a midnight feast.

Draw what was in your picnic basket below:

Date completed: Day ________ Month ________________ Year ____________

43 Learn Morse code

Can you send your name in Morse code?

What you need:

- A torch
- The Morse code alphabet (see below)

Morse code is a mix of dots and dashes. You can use it to communicate in the dark with a torch. Make a dot by switching the torch on and off again quickly. Make a dash by leaving it on for the time it takes to say 'one elephant' in your head.

Write a short message here and try sending it in code:

Top tip!

Say 'one elephant' twice between each letter to make it nice and clear.

A	._	**N**	_.
B	_...	**O**	___
C	_._.	**P**	.__.
D	_..	**Q**	__._
E	.	**R**	._.
F	.._.	**S**	...
G	__.	**T**	_
H	....	**U**	.._
I	..	**V**	..._
J	.___	**W**	.__
K	_._	**X**	_.._
L	._..	**Y**	_.__
M	__	**Z**	__..

Date completed: Day ________ Month ______________ Year ____________

44

Test your night vision

How well can you see in the dark?

What you need:

- An eye chart – take a piece of paper and write 5 random letters in a line. Write 7 more lines with the letters smaller in each one
- Carrots, blueberries and apricots

Top tip!

Being relaxed is very important, so make sure you are warm and not too tired.

Eating foods like carrots, blueberries and apricots, drinking lots of water and moving your eyes from side to side are all ways of helping you see a little better in the dark. Do some of your own experiments using your eye chart to test your improvement over the course of a few nights.

Copy your eye chart here and mark down how well you did:

Date completed: Day ________ Month ________________ Year ____________

45

Howl at the full moon

Tip your head back and let out your wildest howl!

What you need:

- Your voice
- A good howling place

Top tip!

Wait until the full moon for a really powerful howl.

Howling is great fun, especially if you need to let out some energy after doing your homework or tidying your room. Find a good howling place, such as the top of a hill or a wide open space. Tip your head back and let out your longest and loudest howl. Now, doesn't that feel better!

Did you know?

Howling is an important social event for wolves. If one starts howling the others will soon follow.

How did howling make you feel? Write some words to describe your feelings here:

Date completed: Day ________ Month ____________ Year __________

46

Create an ice sculpture

Design an incredible ice sculpture to freeze over night

What you need:

- Water
- Different-shaped balloons
- A small amount of sand

In winter, night-time can get icy cold. Take a balloon, put a tablespoon of sand in it and fill it with water before tying the top. Shape these balloons to create your sculpture. Pile them on top of each other or curve long thin ones around trees. The next morning you will be able to peel the balloon away, revealing your sculpture beneath.

Top tip!

Use a little food colouring or some natural treasures in the water to make a fascinating multi-coloured ice sculpture.

Take a photo of your ice sculpture and stick it here:

Date completed: Day ________ Month ______________ Year ___________

47 Record the sunset

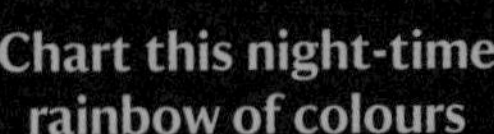

Chart this night-time rainbow of colours

What you need:

- A piece of paper
- Oil pastels, crayons or coloured pencils

The colour of a sunset is created by tiny specks of dust in the air. As these are constantly changing, there will never be two sunsets the same. Use the table below to record a week of sunsets. Each evening, find a crayon which best matches the colour of the sunset.

Top tip!

If there is more than one colour, record them all or use oil pastels and your thumb to blend them together.

Monday ______________________

Tuesday ______________________

Wednesday ______________________

Thursday ______________________

Friday ______________________

Saturday ______________________

Sunday ______________________

Date completed: Day ________ Month ______________ Year __________

48

Draw a sensory map

Rely on all your senses to create this night-time map

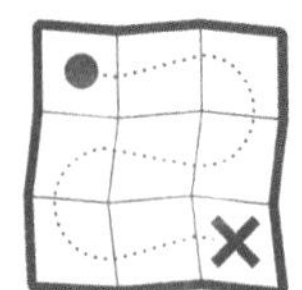

What you need:

- A torch
- A piece of paper
- A pencil
- Warm clothes

Take a paper and pencil on a familiar walk in the dark. Use your senses to create a map as you go – mark the special smells, sounds and textures. You can light the way using your torch if you need to. Be sure to check what you are touching first and never touch anything that looks poisonous or like it may hurt you.

Top tip!

Go back during the day and see if you can follow your map.

Draw a copy of your sensory map here:

Date completed: Day ________ Month ______________ Year ___________

49 Plant a night garden

Create a garden that's at its best when the sun goes down

What you need:

- A grow bag or flower bed

One or all of the following:

- A packet of night-scented stock seeds
- A packet of night phlox seeds
- A packet of evening primrose seeds

Some plants flower or release their scent at night to attract nocturnal creatures such as moths. Find a patch of garden and sow seeds for some of the plants above. Check the back of the packet for directions.

Top tip!

Night-scented stock is particularly easy to grow, but it keeps low to the ground. Put it at the front of a flower bed or in a pot.

Draw a picture of your night garden here:

Date completed: Day ________ Month ________________ Year ____________

50

Discover a natural night-time wonder

Can you see the milky way or a meteor shower?

What you need:

- A tip from the internet, news or a friend
- The right place at the right time

Spotting a natural night-time wonder is a mixture of luck and good timing. The milky way can be seen on clear nights in places far away from street lights. We can often predict when a meteor shower will happen, so have a look on the internet or listen out on the news to know when to look. The best ones are in August (the Perseids) and November (the Leonids).

What night-time wonders did you spot?

Top tip!

Giving your eyes some time to adjust to the darkness will help you to be able to focus on the night sky, so make sure you are outside for at least half an hour.

Did you know?

Meteors are pieces of rock or ice often no bigger than a grain of sand burning as they hit the Earth's atmosphere.

Date completed: Day ________ Month ________________ Year ____________

1
2
3
4

10 BEST Things to Do

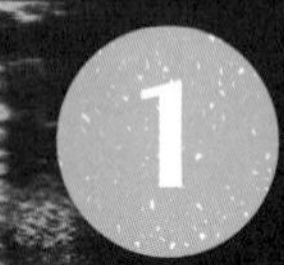

Cook campfire popcorn (page 17)

Poke a needle and string through any plain unsalted popcorn that's left over and hang it in your garden as a brilliant snack for wild birds. Add dried fruit as an extra treat for them.

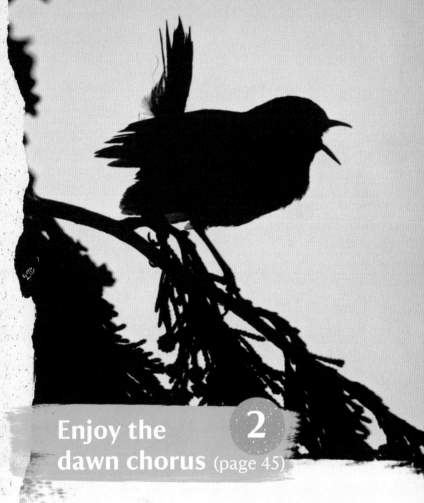

Enjoy the dawn chorus (page 45)

2

If you enjoy the dawn chorus, why not listen to the dusk chorus too? Blackbirds and song thrushes love to sing as it gets dark. If you're really lucky, you might be able to hear nightjars and nightingales. They are both tricky to find, so contact your local birdwatching group to find out the best places.

Light up a snow lantern (page 35)

3

Once you master building snow lanterns you can get more creative. Try adding a ball of snow on top and decorating it with a face to create a snowman with a glowing belly!

4

Become a night rider
(page 49)

To be safe, don't ride on roads at night and never go alone. The Highway Code has lots of great advice on keeping safe, as well as some of the laws you should know about when you are riding. When it was first published in 1931, it cost just one penny, now you can get it for free online.

5 Play on a moonlit beach (page 54)

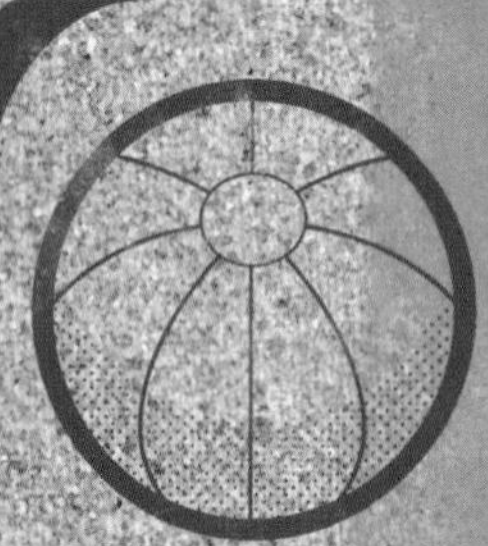

Why not do some night-time sand sculpting? Have a competition to make the tallest sand lighthouse and top it off with a torch or a tea light. One of the Seven Wonders of the Ancient World was a lighthouse, the Pharos of Alexandria in Egypt. Records tell us that it was 137 metres tall and had an open fire at the top.

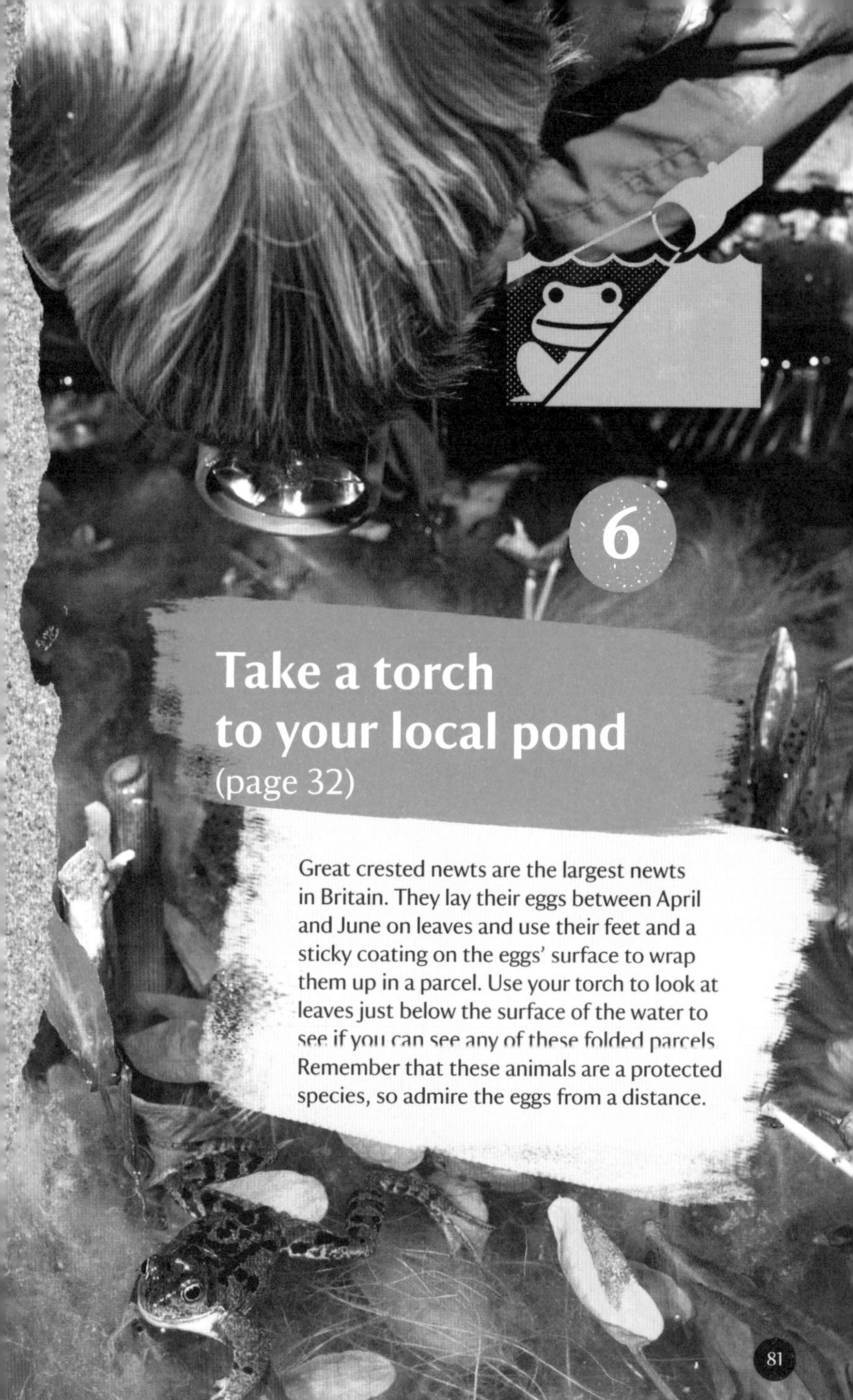

6

Take a torch to your local pond

(page 32)

Great crested newts are the largest newts in Britain. They lay their eggs between April and June on leaves and use their feet and a sticky coating on the eggs' surface to wrap them up in a parcel. Use your torch to look at leaves just below the surface of the water to see if you can see any of these folded parcels. Remember that these animals are a protected species, so admire the eggs from a distance.

Create a feast for a hedgehog (page 22)

7

Remember that hedgehogs hibernate from around November until April, so save your hog feast until you know it will be appreciated. During hibernation their heart rate drops from 190 to 20 beats per minute, which helps them to survive longer on the fat reserves from the food they ate before winter.

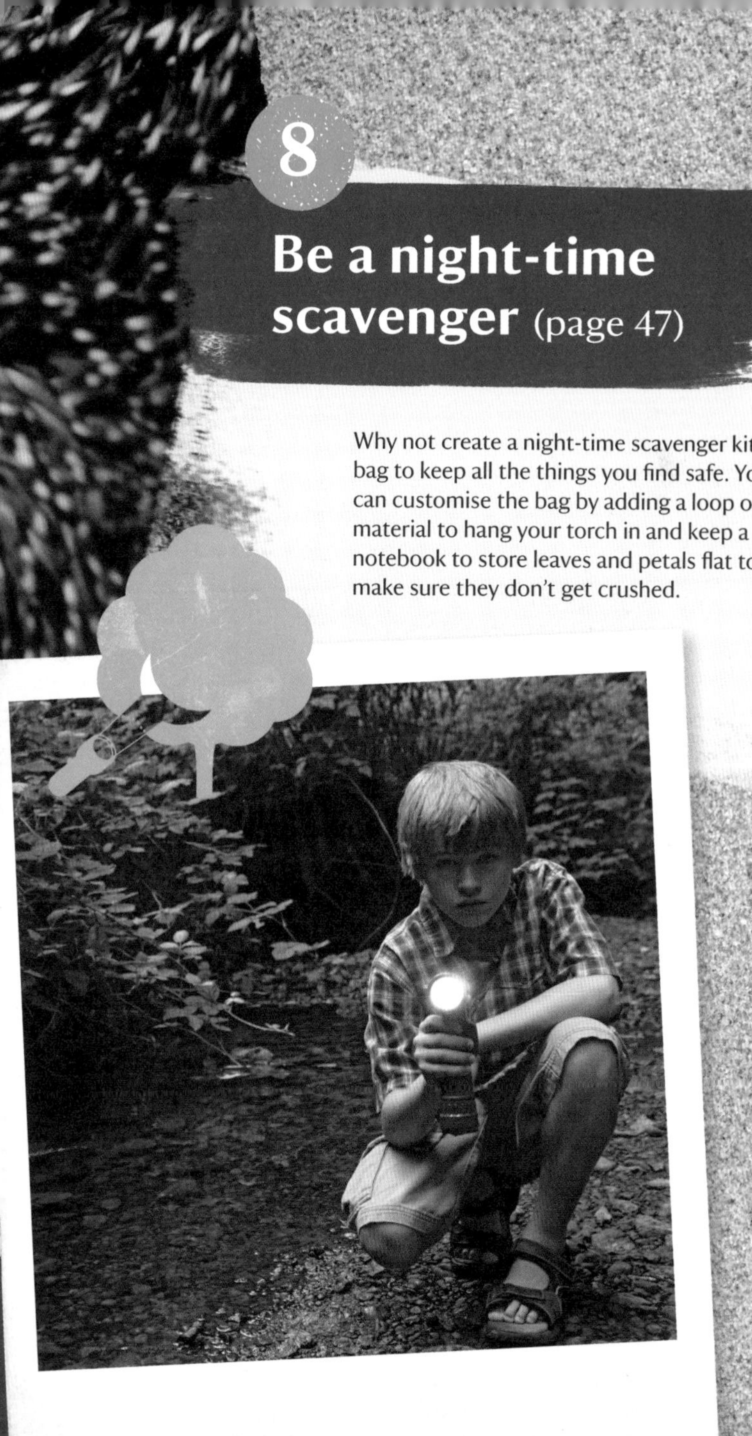

8

Be a night-time scavenger (page 47)

Why not create a night-time scavenger kit bag to keep all the things you find safe. You can customise the bag by adding a loop of material to hang your torch in and keep a notebook to store leaves and petals flat to make sure they don't get crushed.

9

Create a new constellation (page 59)

Many of the constellations are named after Greek and Roman characters in stories. The Greeks would act out these stories wearing masks. Tell your constellation story by making your own masks and acting it out using the glow of the tea lights as your stage lighting.

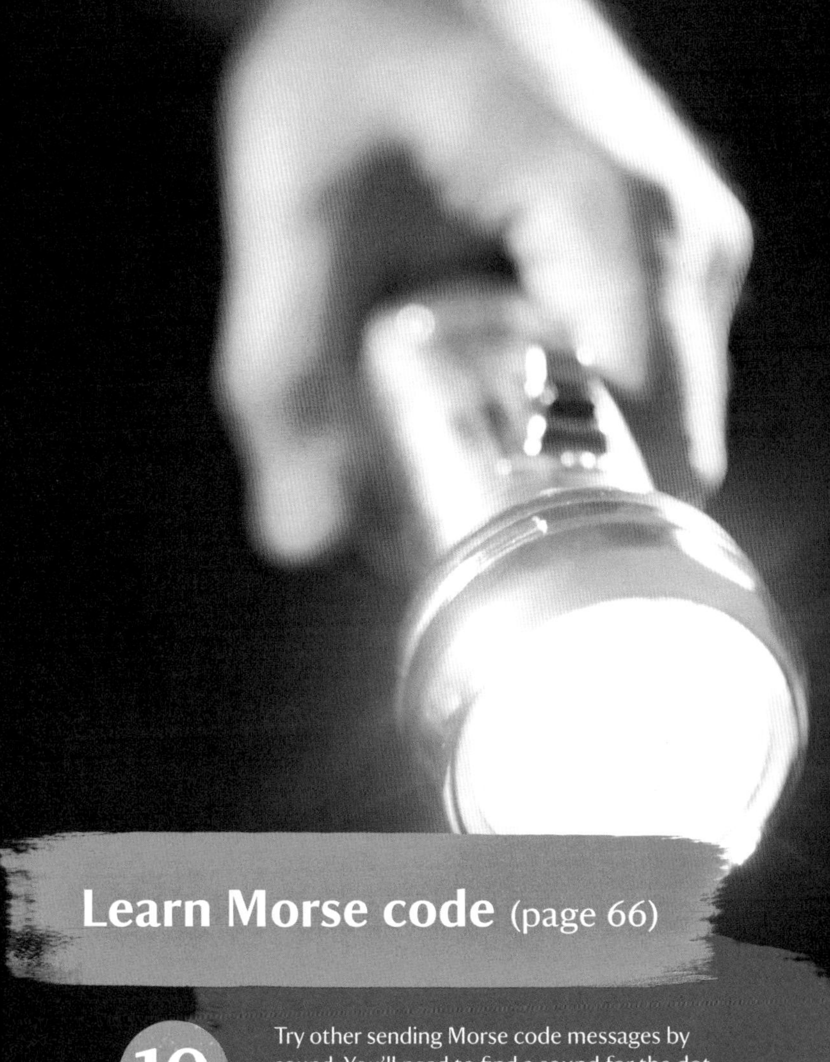

Learn Morse code (page 66)

10

Try other sending Morse code messages by sound. You'll need to find a sound for the dot and a different one for the dash. Perhaps tap a tree trunk for the dot and scrape the bark for the dash.

5 best things to do in

SPRING

5 Set up a moth trap

Did you know?

There are over 2400 different species of moths in the UK and just 59 species of butterfly. Butterflies and moths belong to a group of animals called *Lepidoptera*, which comes from the Greek for 'scaley winged'.

49 Plant a night garden

Did you know?

Plants that have white or pale flowers will look especially beautiful under a full moon, as they reflect the moonlight. This helps some insects to see them in the dark.

25 Search for eyes in the dark

Did you know?

Reflective markings on roads are called cat's eyes. This is because the inventor, Percy Shaw, was inspired by the reflection from the eyes of cats when light was shone on them at night.

19 Become a moongazer

Did you know?

From Earth we always see the same side of the moon. The other side is completely hidden from us!

42 Have a picnic in the dark

Did you know?

Try packing your picnic for each other. That way, when you eat it in the dark, you've no idea what to expect. You can give diners a clue by using smelly ingredients such as pickle, flavoured crisps and oranges.

5 best things to do in

SUMMER

13

Go on a bat walk

Did you know?

There are 18 species of bat in the UK. The noctule bat is the biggest, but it's still smaller than the palm of your hand!

33

Play on a moonlit beach

Did you know?

How high or low the tide is can be affected by the time of year and the time of the month, so don't trust where the tides came to last time you played. It may be very different next time. Look online for tide timetables, as these will give you exact timings of high and low tides each day.

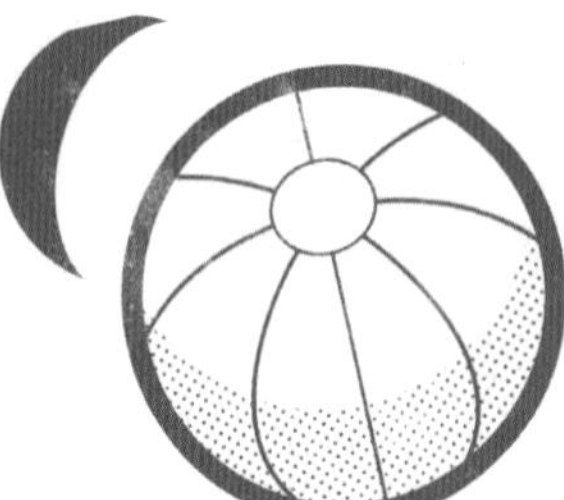

24 Sleep under the stars

Did you know?

Even in the summer it can get chilly at night. Warm up before you get into bed by doing star jumps and running about. A lot of the heat in your body can escape from your head so wear a wooly hat too.

21 Search for glow worms

Did you know?

Adult glow worms cannot eat. They live for about 14 days, mate and lay eggs then die. This means they spend most of their life as larvae.

Record the sunset 47

Did you know?

Have you ever heard of the phrase 'Red sky at night, shepherd's delight'? It suggests that a red sunset means the next day will bring good weather. Try using your sunset chart to find out if this is really true.

5 best things to do in

AUTUMN

12 Keep an eye on fungi

Did you know?

Some fungi actually glow in the dark! The most common one in this country is the honey fungus, which grows on rotting wood. It has its name because it smells like honey.

6 Hollow out a Punkie Night lantern

Did you know?

The inside of a Punkie lantern can be delicious roasted with some butter, herbs and a tiny bit of honey.

4

Have a bonfire

Top Tip

Nature can provide fantastic firelighters. Try finding a hard fungus called King Alfred's Cake on dead trees. They look like little black buns and make great kindling.

7

Create a feast for a hedgehog

Did you know?

Hedgehogs eat lots of slugs, which also usually come out at night when it is cooler and damper. If you are a keen gardener, a hedgehog in your garden will help keep slug numbers down. But remember not to use slug pellets down because they could poison the hedgehogs too.

11

Tell the time using the moon

The problem with trying to tell the time using the sun or the moon is that you can only estimate to the nearest hour or so. Try guessing the length of a minute. Do this in the dark and do it in a lit place to see if the light changes your ability to guess.

5 best things to do in WINTER

36 Tell stories by firelight

Did you know?

Tell a story you know really wel. The best storytellers know their stories off by heart. That way you can act parts of the story to bring it to life and even change parts of it to suit your audience, like including them as characters or setting it around a bonfire.

46 Create an ice sculpture

Add the natural objects picked up on your scavenger hunt to the water in the balloons to display them in your amazing ice sculpture.

39 Make a scary forest

Did you know?

If you fill a glass bottle with water and blow across the top you can make fantastic howling noises. Try to have someone hidden in the undergrowth doing this as you lead your friends on their scary walk.

29 Go wassailing

Did you know?

Here are a few lines from an old Wassail Song to get you started:
'Here we come a-wassailing
Among the leaves so green,
Here we come a-wandering
So fair to be seen.'
Can you make up the next verse?

50 Discover a natural night-time wonder

If this gives you a taste for amazing night-time events, look up the next lunar eclipse. This only happens when the sun, moon and earth all line up perfectly. Sometimes during an eclipse the moon even glows red.

Checkpoint Charlie

Well done, Night-time Adventurers, you have completed all 50 challenges!

Write down which one made you feel:

the most BRAVE

....

the most EXCITED

....

the most SILLY

....

the most SNEAKY

....

the most MESSY!

....